Modulations

Poems by

Richard Martin

Paradise / Asylum Arts / 1998

Acknowledgments

Some of these poems have first appeared in the following magazines:
ACM; Asylum Annual; Caprice; Café Review; Colorado North Review; Estuaires;
Exquisite Corpse; Fell Swoop; 5 A.M.; Mesechabe; Mike & Dale & Hoa's Younger
Poets; MSS/New Myths; Pulpsmith; Red Brick Review; Rolling Stone.

Thanks also to Peter Kidd at Igneus Press for publishing the chapbook
Negation Of Beautiful Words in which some of these poems first appeared.

"Proper Ventilation" first appeared in the anthology Aloud: Voices From the
Nuyorican Poets Cafe, Henry Holt, 1994. Thanks as well to editors Miguel
Algarin and Bob Holman.

This book is dedicated to Tom H., Joel, and Eileen.

ISBN 1-878580-67-1

Library of Congress Catalog Number : 98-73282

Book and cover design by Greg Boyd
Cover painting by Tom Haines

Asylum Arts
5847 Sawmill Road
Paradise, CA 95969

Contents

Modulations

Listening To The Radio

The mosque next door
meets Wyatt Earp.

The old liberal
finds
enough coins
on the living room
rug
to buy a
pack of cigarettes.

Pass
the verb tense
please!

Across the deck
wind stirs
leaves and paper bags.

The first flower
of mind arrives
in a shower of snow.

The boy is told
to sit up
straight
at his desk.

Stop fidgeting!

Those years
pledging
flags
while cats slept
on the backs
of chairs.

I never did solve
a quadratic equation
or ride the moon
like a yellow metaphor
to the town hall.

Who said the brain
leaps
like a frog
into strong currents
of love?

They built
the military-industrial
complex
didn't they?

New theory states
neutrinos
from an exploding
star caused
the dinosaurs' extinction.

The sacred humor
of knowledge:
lovely rain

on floor
and window sill.

Particulars
always particulars.

The time we stood
under a street lamp
with lipstick
in our hip pockets.

Quarts of milk
dad drank
reading WW2 novels
under a thin light.

Mom snoring
softly
on the couch:
pink curlers
in her hair.

Personal Truth Poem

In the year of my dialectic
I lost most of my hair
and walked around town
with a light bulb in my mouth

I drank constantly

Used colored pencils to juxtapose
graveyards with postmodern delivery rooms
where infants crooned of oceans
blood-red in color

In the year of my dialectic
I swore to banish philosophies
of light and darkness
to celestial spheres more suited
to multiplicities

I drank constantly

Used advanced telecommunications
to speak with disease centers
in my body
overcome by holographic facts
of cellular hysteria

For Two, Please

look   the image in my head
is of a black sun and a can of gravy made of lies
if you say red one and free fall associate
into a can of Chef Boyardee ravioli   how
you ate them everyday as a child   and once
were beaten silly by some playground pals
because of cheddar breath   and how this
incident drove you inside   and made you think
books should be stripped of their covers
that they're nothing more than electronic blips and beeps
on a screen to be arranged by the laptop owner
into the whims and fantasies of his present state
of mind   and so what   because isn't that what the mind
is about anyway   the capacity to branch out
into any kind of silly infinity   at any moment
of object   psychical or physical   and all those
dead debates about the correct critical reading   and how
maybe it's important to be trained for years at heady
universities to understand exactly the valid interpretation
of random words and experiences in the giant brains
of our most important geniuses   have cannonballed
into radical response readers   readers with an itch
for plastic keys and options   readers consuming
and swallowing data like flaming swords   traveling along
the Internet full of hypertext schemes and desires
ready to lock on an image that has nothing to do with
alligators and chameleon coins spinning on the
surface of a raspberry planet which in this poem
occur after lies congealed under rays of darkness
form governments and police departments   not before
a school yard punch in the stomach   bloody tooth
and your mom heating up another can

Blackjack

They anointed his
intelligence
and threw him into
the river
of life
UNFORTUNATE TROPES OF THE WORLD
unite
This is what happens
when I wear my Bruin's
hat
and blondes with nose rings
work the rib grill
LOCAL TIME STAR DATE
the temporal horizon
What if a german
shepherd
took the Heidegger course
with me
Flash of memory
in a cardsharp's
hands

On barroom napkins
TV politicians scribble
violence inflames society
"Do you have a pay phone?"
"Not anymore."
Sweet spontaneity turns
the windows
into lemons

Ten years ago my
   Cousin Fireball
         bought a case
of Anchor Steam
We sat in his backyard
   and launched arrows
         into a neighbor's yard
COGITO ERGO SUM
   Stretch the narrative
into a house of mirrors
   The barrel over
the waterfall leaves
   in ten minutes

DOT DOT DOT
         Morse was
the name of my cub
scout pack's den mother
She took us
      on walks along
the Susquehanna River
   and made us
make pot holders
You can't stop and discuss
the charm
of intertexualtiy
   when someone's chasing
you down the street
   with a wolf badge
   Dad made the backboard
into a table
   and left home
the day my brother beat
him in
ping pong

Domestic Dispute

She tipped over his chair.
He ate an apple and spit the seeds into astronauts.
Those armed with a cliché said a prayer.
The rhododendrons blazed.
A crow in green grass.
Then a man trapped in a theory of form
whirled around in the street.
Black rain fell.

He grabbed her ankles and yanked her from bed.
She ate a banana and put the peel in a safe deposit box.
A friend called and described what she heard:
"It's like an asteroid hitting us," she said.
"When I look out the window I see it
in love with tigers of wind."

Fast Cars

in his brain
grease gods from Detroit
dig holes
and plant trees
with vinyl roots

tenacious
the roots suck
dreams into leaves
shaped like billboards

as advertisements
they display
violent products
to those
driving by
in fast cars

Projection

It turned into a future
of lakes
and this attendant
from an inside wall
of a pyramid
minutes from downtown Cairo.
Alive fresh from stone
to dash
across dreams
the kind you wake up from
after an evening
of booze
and sucker pool
startled
almost breathless
because
of the ghost
a sense
of lobotomy
an exchange of dark heads
rolling
down tunnels
then the flash of light
and when
the eyes adjust
I saw her
naked
white as a potato
passing in front
of me
on her way

to get a glass
of water
for the long
night
in front of us.

This was not
my idea
of future
back then
on that couch
in the city
of in-laws
where I landed
a bird with bullet hole wings
to recite
in a haze of rosaries
the shopping list
of duties
I would perform
via
walls
shadows
fingers rigged
like puppets
when cars
lobbed headlights
into the room
like grenades.
I didn't understand
future
had tired
of the word oblivion
knew the true
apocalypse

stitched in my skin
like flakes
of gold
was a tattoo
that would fade
years later
called beer sign
flamingo
the ankle of elegance
by some
with memories
erased
by elixir tv
and news
of total intoxication.

Elect Me

I have the skin and votes to become
an American hero slash Legend. First
my skin: I burn easily. Walked
around the "old neighborhood" with
a red face, the occasional blister
on the tip of my nose sizzling like
a tiny omelet. No such thing
as sunblock back then. Just
baseballs, fielding grounders
under blue sky. Plenty of radiation.
Without ozone hole etc. Some thoughts
on more than one occasion that
the Sun was the Egyptian God Ra.
Pure Light of God the Father. Heat-
stroke and photosynthetic dreams too:
the one in which green plants e-mail
my holiday plans to weather satellites.
Jumpcut to my hands in the dirt.
The day a friend showed me how
to plant and water lilacs on a rich
man's lawn. The moment I told a woman
in a red party dress that sunlight
cruised through my veins. We were
in a Chinese restaurant next
to tank of large exotic fish.
She squeezed my hand like an orange.
I bit into my lip like a candle flame.
Skipped my next dermatologist appoint-
ment. Parted my hair down the middle
and buzzed like a street light.

There's magic in my proposal for
a midnight sun in every pot. I am
not derivative. I've looked into
the eyes of my neighbors. Studied
the maps of their facial expressions.
I have the votes. I'm burning up.

Clutter

1.

file the lamp shade
under postcards
of light
if you cut down the tree
I will move
WAKE UP
cutthroat useless information
for sale
all these little things
in the mind:
synapse armada of white flags
because I could dance
without stopping
I was awarded the extra hot
barbecue sauce

2.

the pleasure of your mouth
is required
at our next conversation
if it is cancer
it might come back
I don't want to be afraid
of language
the sequence of random thoughts
subtle appeals in the mirror

I didn't mean to enter this stream
where are the scissors
for the jargon collage
"No products but in process."
holy smoke! amigo, my foot is on fire

3.

blatant body
riddled with truth holes
intergalactic genius grants
for the few
and Far Rock Aways'
doors of assimilation
and Tom's renovation
of old buildings
bang bang
deep image encounter
of a lifetime

4.

one whale of a sigh
postexistential tables and chairs
"I was never in despair."
first rung
not knowing you are
who cares for
glamorous orange eyelids
cosmic dust pancakes of self
the inability to come to
a point

nothing divine
divine nothing
position unknown captain
my captain
Pascal's wager
heard about it once
in high school

5.

outside memory banks
thoughts spawn like fish
"Which way did he go, George?"
Making sense of hoola-hoops
and hot dogs on Good Friday
the constant drift
of attention
the what-if ship sailing
into a black hole
time pronounced dead
by the cagey metaphysician
of wait will ya
just for a second

Synthetic Skyline

in short pants
philosophers of artificial intelligence
set books by Hegel on fire
this is what chance conversation is about:
two people on a train
one with diamonds from the heist
in a velvet bag
in a suitcoat pocket
the other reading Kant's
PROLEGOMENA TO A FUTURE METAPHYSICS

how about that "thing in itself"
the thief says lighting his cigar
with a blue finger

close your eyes in the next patch
of sunlight   feel the crackle
of dialectic   the soft
red blanket spread
on green grass in the park
by a man and woman
committed to an afternoon kiss
while ducks float on a still pond

who's saying this, the reader replies
confused when the thief
gets up and heads for the dining car

On The Border Of A Chill

The snow piling up on my skin
reminds the man
trapped in the transfer
of mountains
into bone
of the handkerchief dropped
by a lover
on the night
an errand of bread and milk
turned into a fever.

The body is an old thing:
more clock than memory.
The illusion of moon and horizon
ticks in my fingers.
I know the age of gods and rocks.
I wear their skin.
Dark forms swirl in the blood.

The ceiling spins like a kaleidoscopic top.
A snake coils around my spine.
A voice turns white and falls
into a bucket of wax.
The body is a ritual:
a candle of throats
and things to do.
I see the killer in the pair of pants
and change into feathers.
The bedpost points the gun and fires.

The doctor will come
and make the duck in my stomach
speak in tongues.

The body is street corners and coincidence.
It took years to learn
to sleep like mountains
and dream waterfalls
of bone to climb.
The body is its ancestors:
snap and creak of tree
wind and brittle leaf
the sacred sound of paw
are eggs on stone
as children cry.

Acceleration

I eat in the finest restaurants.

Bacon bit aficionados.

Since my mind broke.

Into three parts.

I laugh at the most inappropriate times.

There was a time.

Before my golf handicap.

The hospital refused.

A simple aspirin.

For my painful gut.

Now it's winter.

And I'm alone.

In the frozen stares of others.

This is not "that".

I heard once.

At a wagon wheel convention.

On decay.

When my friend.

Hopped a donkey.

And rode deep.

Into a canyon of dancers.

I stepped on the gas.

To lose my watch.

A Man In Dublin

A man loads the index finger of his right hand
with pantomime bullets. In parks
flowers receive pollen from yellow bees.
There is an imaginary knife tucked inside his pants.
A loud goose is upset with a green pond.
On his belt he clips plastic grenades.
Lovers kiss on a famous bridge. Sudden urine
flows from city statues.
The man is up for a good time.
The bathroom mirror retains his grin.
Pigeons have red feet.
It is a friend from childhood.
Made from the sadness he saw in old comedians.
Soot on stone buildings is called black lace.

The man's hands are made of dirt. In the backseat
of an empty car silence is defined.
A dark clown in his brain wants a drink.
The sea deposits grey words on endless shores.
When there is work it ends in long lines for waiting.
Smoke trails move across the sky.
This time the man is in Dublin.
Tomorrow he'll be seen in Pittsburgh.
Surface like a beached whale in central Ohio.
In Beijing he'll light a cigarette outside of McDonald's.
Now he walks down Baggot Street.

The clown's thirst is full of bears. It was
a tough week on the streets. Balloons flew
into sea gulls with wings of fire.

Jokes got trapped beneath the wheels of black cars.
The red nose smelled bad.   The man
refused to practice his moves.
Open the door when nobody's there.
Close it on a crowd of questions.
Move inside glass.
Kill the neighbor with funny lips.
I need a drink goddamn it.
The man steps on sparse shadows.
Beggars with their backs to the moon.

There has to be victims.
Inside a pub he listens to men play Irish blues.
He understands a red face is a stoic expression.
He shouts at fingers to move faster.
A violin leaps past the history of sheep on sheer ridges.
The man grins.   Swigs his Guinness.
The pub reflects the fate of conversation.
Stars shutter.   Grenades explode.

Paradise

This morning
the eternal body visits
the car wash.
After that
it's time to pick up the kids
and make them tacos.
The grass is kind of long
and the phone company claims
it's time to disconnect the phone.
On the short list: weeds poking
through the steps of the porch.
Hosta plotting to take over the
flower bed. New concerns
about spontaneity.
New edition of automatic history
        to peruse.
        The time "the wife"
forgot to set out the argyle socks.
New Age music.
New American writing.
"Make it new."
Why others in the office
        receive appropriate promotions.
Idyllic dreams: the one
        in which the eternal body
wanders around a lake
        with a bow and arrow.
The time the fax machine
        filled the room
        with fresh green leaves
gifts for the poor
        the glass of champagne.

Certain Betrayals

The woman on the blue horse
        hands
a bouquet of sheet music
to the man
        walking
backwards on the railroad tracks

The jazz of randomness
        buys
a new hat and
        bops
into a circle of nouns

The ants
    go marching
into a rose of sounds

        Leave
the ingredients for the borrowed cake
on the night stand
next to the Sacred Heart

The censor of Imagination
        maintains
all hearts are sacred

The fear of leaping into the unknown
        guides
the pencil up a ladder of light

No hedging of bets
we
  are
divine
but
  prefer
to take our time with simple insights

The stand of bare trees
a snowflake
a road becoming dirt and dust
  sing
like cute warblers of pain

Too easy the clown of diction
  admonishes
the window washers

Pumpkins of form
New words
  asked
to step inside the particle accelerator

The shadow of my hand on the flickering page

   Unconscious boats
    adrift
   in a collage of raindrops

  This way to escape intention

  Make-up tests on the half-shell

Rocks & Tubas

He acts strange.
He complains
When his mouth
Is dry & desires wet food.
Neighbors realize this.
He bothers us
They cry when their dogs
Mistake sirens
For Easter eggs.
His dreams involve
Etymologies that travel
Too close to the sun.
He has the power
To assemble sounds
Into rocks & tubas.
When he appears
At his window
Dictionary in hand
Everyone hides behind
Television sets.
It is unsafe
When he carves
The pronunciation key
Onto a hand
Or utters a new word
Round & hard
As a golf ball.

The Difference Between
Used Cars And Language

Seaweed
and
the new graffiti of waves
splash over my feet
Downtown
the young maestro strums a yellow guitar
and
dreams of the V-8 engine
The country moves like a hurricane into itself
Cans of laughter
and
reels of mistakes later
the history teacher takes off his shoes
The rest is tv
The way it talks about itself
what it's up to during this period of gimmicks
and power
On an ice floe my favorite etymologist straps three words
a red scarf
and
a band-aid
The content miser shaves in a froth of form
hallelujah
Vowels in the waiting room of the lung hospital
appear ready to escape
histrionics
There's sunlight on my dancing hand
hallucinate
Deep in the alley poets decide on pick-up-sticks

or
the I Ching
Give a listen to the bells and tolling clouds
"Come on down and drive this baby,
if you don't believe the flashing odometer!"
In a series of blue don't cross out blue
As far as new worlds . . .
Close your eyes
and
count to ten
Capture the flag
Jump from roof to roof in your neighborhood
Applaud the sounds spinning around dissolved objects
Kiss the tree anyway

Modulations

they want voice not multiple selves
tuned into their favorite
radio stations   lots of static
maybe bananas this morning   how about
them baseball players   how they
mumble "fly ball" and "heads up"
for mom's apple pies   the point of all
transmission is quick transcription   then
off for a day on the boat of pure sensation
cesura   cesura   cesura   cesura   cesura
some enjambment and toe clippings
for professors   as for waves
giant green ones through empty mind
o big blue sky just like my hat

Into The Yellow Darkness

I need to be drugged and running a marathon

I love our stories of pumpkins
and ladders to the moon

Today was a tough day for everybody at the office

The president seems to gloat
when he walks

It's history after all
and the reviews of bloodshed
must cease

This is the way of consciousness
not Tao
though I love it like a vanilla
popsicle

Spin-offs and spin-cycles
it still feels good to stretch out
on the bed
take a deep breath
and not hurt the eyes

I am falling apart and building something
out of that

The beach is down the street
down the road
across from over there

And the convict loose in the neighborhood
is called Houdini
by the secretary who worries
about computer screen lights

Remember the radon scare
How a shower equalled a pack of cigarettes

Now schools don't open on time
because of asbestos
and a secret memo
from one assistant superintendent to another
claims lead is worse

There is no time to start a short story
If there was

maybe a first line like:

"After the imagination festival, we drove back to Jerry's
and dropped acid."

That's how my senses opened
By the third page
I was on the street and staring
at a lilac in full bloom
The blood through my heart
like a warm-up band

That's what prose is all about

And there are plenty of dreams
where the whales return
and don't forget the humpback we saw
30 yards before the bow
it breached into our lives forever

Remember our hysterical laughter

Remember how perfect the ladder
lay against the moon

Beanstalk and all in our heads
we climbed
out of time
out of space
out of anything to say
We went up and up
into the yellow darkness

Preachers

The preachers of divine harmony
have just been murdered
by the preachers of ultimate war.

You had to have cable tv
to witness it.

The preachers of ultimate war
have just been murdered
by very poor ratings.

It says so right here
in TV Guide.

File Cabinets

Right out of the Trinity
they arrive
in bright blue suits.
They have the jobs
prayed for in Catholic grammar schools.
They were the esoteric ones
who didn't become
used car salesmen or drunks
with red-rough faces.
They had to have imagination
to envision the number of toilets
flushed in a minute.
They were the pets and laughed
at those possessed by demons.

They keep track of things:

mothballs
paper clips
telephone numbers
secret thoughts
disaster plans

you name it
just so nothing slips
into the giant hole
that eats what it wants
when it wants.

The brightest one asks me
how many file cabinets
there are in the office.

I see two and say: "Two."
"How many memos in each
would you say?"
"Rough estimate?"
"Sure."
"Well, let's see. I write
a dozen a minute
and have been on the job for nine months."

This intrigues the lizard.
Paper is a major expenditure
for a small company.
He reaches for a pocket calculator
that plays Brahms
when it is time for him
to touch his lonely balls.

In a moment
unable to control his spit
he yells:
"A MILLION MEMOS!"
"Five hundred thousand in each cabinet," I say.
"ON WHAT!   ON WHAT!"

His buddies are pretty excited
and make no bones
zipping their flies up and down
like a Chinese woman
fingering beads on an abacus.

"ON WHAT!   ON WHAT!"

My boss is nervous and digs
a serpent from his eye
with a nail clipper.

"ON WHAT!   ON WHAT!"

"On death
jerks
ON DEATH
always on death."

Disc Full Samsara

blue screams in the funky basket
"A" my name is asteroid
and I voice the original error

time is my polliwog buddy
dear mother:
I know the words for sky

out there
my sense of criticism
involved in sensation

It's called entering the recall button
forced and forsaken
on the knoll of gunslingers

a way to evade the politics
of common speech
the steeplechase morning

in sagging body
o please doctor of pawn
hear my song

Rubric

4

Four blondes smoking cigarettes under a fall lamp
Syntax is complex
Superheated coffee cups imitating dawn
Style unique & appropriate to purpose
A bouquet of high-heels on brick sidewalks
Stays focused on topic
Eyes shift into red cabs
Use of high frequency words
Full of office products buildings linger without tasks
Details fit where they belong
Zero in on rivers
Tone appropriate & controlled
Copper leaves snap in a stiff wind
Awareness of audience
Palms of gold

3

Three brunettes smoking cigarettes by a small lamp
Syntax is fairly complex
Heated coffee cups imitating dawn
Style unique & fits purpose
A bouquet of pumps on brick sidewalks
Focused on topic
Eyes follow red cabs
Use of high frequency words
Full of office products buildings languish without tasks
Details fit where they belong

Zero in on tributaries
Tone appropriate & monitored
Russet leaves drift in the wind
Awareness of audience
Palms of gold

2

Two redheads smoking cigarettes with a flashlight
Syntax is nearly complex
Warm coffee cups imitate dawn
Style stolen & feigns purpose
A bouquet of saddle shoes on brick sidewalks
Unfocused topic
Eyes hop into red cabs
Use of swear words
Full of office products buildings vanish into tasks
Details flit where they belong
Zero in on creeks
Tone brash & free
Leaves drift in the wind
Awareness of audience
Palms of gold

1

One black-haired beauty smoking a cigarette
Syntax is recklessly simple
Coffee cup imitates dawn
Style without purpose
A bouquet of slippers on brick sidewalks
Unknown topic
Eyes like red cabs

Use of erotic words
Full of office products buildings crumble
Details slip where they belong
Zero in on raindrops
Tone whispered into ear
Drift in the wind
Awareness
Gold

Inside

The full presence of life
knocks inside my head
like a fistful
of bodies.

Who am I?

The past.

My eyes mingle with shut
there's drift.

Birch leaf
now yellow
image drops from tree
branch
into space

swirl
scoot of wind

touches lake
see it
rippled face

others
pieces of skin
weird stamps
stuck
between heel
and sole

small armada
formed
above weeds
flickering stones
school of carp
(what are they meeting for)
dart away.

I want to say
two bodies
then four
then eight
inside of me.

NanoSermon

Crows on a treadmill
of white pine

A delicious buzz in my head

Pink flowers
of the rhododendron

Rainburn

for Melissa

Something about the resurrection
of the body

A way of planting flowers
in a downpour
from a tropical depression
lingering off the coast
with a Russian name

The great weight of our trade agreements
Not listening to the talk
of the mind
but placing hands into green soil

And she said she gave up
on her drive for immortality
early in life
that she was undecided about the soul
and then a comment
about Aristotle as a plant . . .
a flowering plant

Meanwhile while sorting
fragments of joy
into a meaningful paradox
we renewed our commitment
to stomp through puddles

How easy it was to tan
in the charming cascade

Saints Without Photo ID's

1

Thinking about the color
   of the brain   pitchers of beer
on all the tables
      Let them be round   and
those drinking from pewter mugs
      quote Chaucer
                  and dream the jigsaw
         puzzles of dawn
So I say to her:
            the woman inside of me
   is a girl
   dressed in plaid jumper
      patent leather shoes
         white socks turned over
         at the ankle
This great distance
            between images
                        the movie
            we watched the
            other night
   with underwater chandeliers
The purpose of purposelessness
            easy transition
         to laughter and feeling good
      about things
The message now spinning like
                  a top
            tipped like a particle
            into vast velocity

hold fast
hold on tight
          the white knuckle
               moment
   of tie clasps and
               cummerbunds
is being built
          out in the barn
  by an aged craftsman
working in pine and shoeshine

2

          Raise your hand
          if you are or ever wanted to be
          a housewife   sunlight
          dialogues of pen and shame
          stories told: blown in doctrines
          of God and technology —
          the shopping list

3

Space   Silence   Beauty

Mystery   Magic   Breath

Here   Now   Is

4

He majored in figments and
dust

5

Never did find work
in a reliquary

6

The atmosphere sweet with birds
and melting snow
A good lather of sweat on the back
cold toes
the industry of energy envisioning
anticipated blossoms
    all colors

Good Words

Rolling in dirt and sunlight
the cat plays
like my eyes
wide
in a stand of birch trees

I've been reading THE
GNOSTIC GOSPELS
by Elaine Pagels
"gnosis"
is a good word
for self-knowledge
"gnocchi"
is a good word
for potato pasta

How many jars
of suppressed manuscripts
still buried in the earth

If the mind is a boomerang
of light
        into darkness . . .

The last time I had them
with my brother at Emile's
I needed extra strength Tums

I'm no authority or disciple
of bureaucracy
the squeeze is on
so open the millennium curtains

The reflection of these trees
this morning
in still water
ears ringing with chipmunks

Hello, who's there
my favorite association

Abandonment

for Bill Parker

I am going out
into the morning sun

There are piles
of leaves
to walk through

A history of birdsong
to record

Look
I've had enough of
the dilemma of buildings

Ceilings don't fit my head
Walls are too tight
around the hips

I can't concentrate
I was born to waste time

On a mission
of detours and asides
I am too a cloud
Don't say
I'm not

My nights are rivers
My dreams are oceans
There's plenty of evaporation
and condensation

You've heard
the rain of my love
striking roofs
and windows

Down lanes of frost
up hills of chilled light
I wander
without information
or goals for the next century

An orphan of open space
I grow like a tree
out of a broken watch

All Is Misunderstanding

She thinks I'm the Buddha
because my belly
pops over my belt buckle

I tell her
it's from 20 yrs. of drinking

She likes to take off
her clothes
and run around the apartment
screaming: Buddha Buddha

I don't deserve
this
Some think
I'm lying
or just plain stupid

Buddha Buddha
she screams

Sadness Competition

All those dropped on their heads
punched in the mouth
deprived of food
and clothing
hit by plates
and flying objects

line up over here

Those kicked from homes
had their land stolen
been relocated
incarcerated
tortured
made to disappear

stand over here

Rape
incest
abuse

here

Those injured or maimed in wars
police actions
on the streets

this line

Famine victims
survivors of holocausts

political prisoners
hostages
biological
chemical
fallout guinea pigs

to the right

Alone
sick
forgotten
addicted
from broken homes
outcasts
disadvantaged

to the left

Have we missed anyone?

The dead?

anywhere

OK the object
is to disclose
fathom cause
mobilize

Our judge today is Time

Everyone wins

Contact High

The world in the back of my head
is out of time   crush the ice symphony
with pathetic toes   don't strain or hesitate
at the unlocked door   step in and out of
velvet lampshade underwear

There are no mistakes
in the story of dunking doughnuts
into coffee   the plague of automatic glass
shatters   the cop on his beat stares at dirt
the laughter in the aisles is for a zebra
with its hoof in the till

It's time to dress up in macaroni and tile
the obscure vocation of waiting   more
unmuffled motorcycles and less alcohol
in the pinched eyes of the damned   what
a week for the hot dog   the news stand
burns a hole in the sky

The victims of forced consciousness
play on a boulevard of words   the fat general
sits on stick of declawed cats
the ends of the universe tune a fiddle
of conjecture   it's time to swap spoons
release the air raid of wet kisses

Balmy Lips

Who could have predicted the perfect mall
a place where all of us would go
to buy and sell
the bits of language still left on our tongues:
blue sky
child
warm day
for December

• • •

Kiss me honey
you make me hot

• • •

Look at the world twirling like a fish
in a cameraman's eyes
O the spin of image and fact
the tacky jargon posted on the refrigerator:
Check out OS2 Warp
Oz is Dead
Pentium chips and mugs
of your favorite right-wing fat mouth
on sale
in time for Christmas

• • •

I licked your breasts
during the pledge of allegiance

• • •

Transmissions come and go
it's part of an alien culture
pill of paranoia
the reward for being a good citizen
Let's not strain here
pull groin or stomach muscle
to show
the page is a business of space and signs

• • •

The money I make
is for your
sexual wardrobe

• • •

It's not like I never met a philosopher
I've known plenty of them
dirt under nails
holes in pants and shoes
always up for a shot and a beer
addicted to horizon and chance
the play of clocks
in the lovely eyes of lost women

the constant jokes and blubber of reputation
I
wash and wax my car
collage my mind with sprinklers and bad debts
so you know
I know what's going on

• • •

O bend me twist me
lilt of legs
hem of dress

• • •

The prison of fettered conversation.
"There's so little to celebrate today."
Something about Worchestershire sauce.
"Talk about heavy duty!"
Saying we can't help ourselves.
In this case.
"That's a different case."
Joy of living.
"I'm sorry — not crazy enough."
Reminded every day not to let the bastards get you.
"That's what you're saying?
They tell me you look great."
Lots of time. We can't. We try to wake up and say hmmm.
"That's the way he looked at things."
I can remember one time — shortly such a — the only time — there is.
"She's in that department?"
Big girl. Joy of the morning.
"I noticed your secretary . . ."

Too bad . . .
"One hand . . ."
Happiness is . . .
"That's right . . ."
At some point . . .
"Kind of . . ."
That way you have to appreciate what you've got.
"Not a very friendly man."
57 when he died.

• • •

She poured out of her sex outfit
she was a flood of flesh

• • •

It was a time in which famous people were shot and killed
a time of great environmental catastrophes
skies darkened by reactor mishaps
young children wandering streets on uranium legs
Debates . . . on and on
A cold war came and went
A time that smelled of oil and cigarettes
of nameless politicians
who lived in a white space
surrounded by fire
and death
who told the poor to get off
their butts
to control sexual organs
who screamed like preachers
about family

and work
in their rat-lever techno-industries

• • •

Kiss me
over and over again

Ideas

sweetly inaudible
when the wind moves a face
towards flowers

Form

Sing

Scrap

Metal

Ocean

Wave

Of

A

Bird

To

The

New

Collapse

Plastic Flowers

for Bern Mulligan

day   ticks of sun
what pants should I wear   a squirrel in the yard
I'll be late for the interview   if I could find my center
fragments & phrases   hip designers & ads
without words   the great metaphors everyone loves
the description of place written on the back
of a postage stamp   mistake
& subsequent diatribe   on the structure
of various prisons   Pot Pot à la Beckett
the universality of the specific   particular   the obscure
"obfuscation" now that's a great word   after
days of rain   glorious fog for the halo of feet
the cat & her patch of sunlight   the way my toes dig
                                    into sand
sound of surf   aquamarine waves   the gull
with broken wing   those jellyfish she hates floating
in the oily harbor   will it help if I align
myself with the holes of criticism   punt on third down   PRO-
SAIC BANAL PROZAC REVERIES FOR EVERYONE   Pierre
Reverdy   the colors of the splendid hat
coming home to roost   what everyone's up to
thinking about   when they pass the remote
to a friend   in some circles it's passé to time
the poem with a stopwatch   long windedness rehearsed
the dictionary in front of my lucky mirror   I was
against allusion   took it on the chin for hyperbole
still lapis lazuli lazily ruled   in my house of blues

Participation

Ten thousand mystics
with all day lollipops
stuck in their ears
march down Main Street
to the yellow bank.

What happens next
is up to you.

In This Corner

The hangover arrives
in clodhoppers
and boxing gloves
it uppercuts the head
and stomps groin

below the belt, ref
what's the matter — you blind
hey, I had your mother last night

The hangover pounds
the body
works it good
then back to the face
take that pretty boy

what an animal

again and again
it attacks
a cut opens near the eye

man, this guy is a bleeder
hangs on the ropes

The hangover lands
punch after punch

what technique
what skills

there's a shot
to the back of the neck
the groin again

who said kicking was allowed
and what about the bell
the fucking bell

The Bartender In 1968

for my father

He says he got the huge forearms
pulling cases off the Coke truck
after the family decided by unanimous vote
there was not time for college
in a house without a father
and mouths to feed
even if he did excel in History and Latin.
Then along comes Hitler and Japan
and he's in the Navy
running a black market scam
in the turret
of one of the big guns
on one of the big ships in the Pacific —
you know cigarettes and cold beer
for the guys and their nerves
watching for nutcase Japs
on kamikaze runs.
He likes to repeat the story
of daring a friend
to dive off the bow with him —
the port in sight —
a thirty-story plunge into water
and he sees his buddy's hair turn white
as he pours another brandy
and sips beer from a short glass.
When the pubescent customers
stoned on pot
tripping on acid
call him old man, baldy, a real asshole
he walks around the bar
clears a couple of stools

bends down and grabs a steel leg
with each hand.
With an exertion that pops the veins
out in his neck
and turns on red bulbs in his face
he jerks the stools
like leaning towers of Pisa
into the air
and with a grunt and dirty smile
slowly brings them back down to the floor
and asks:
"Who in here wants to deal with this?"

Quandaries

Someone's eating my shirt
and stuffing my socks

with garbage.
Clocks tick

and those at the office
discuss the size of the claws

on tv.
Coyote is stupid and drops

the idea of death
in the drinking water.

Coyote is bright and steals
the mouth of the president.

Meanwhile the red apple
rolls into a sonic dream.

The cosmos is chaos and the winos rejoice.
I would like to scream

with a chorus of bafflers
the brain's wiring won't support

a trombone of wintry birds.
The men in the yard

swear by long shovels
they're digging for words.

Because I was handled like meat
grilled onto ceilings

and fried off floors
I have things on my mind

like lost notebooks
when I piss on my leg.

Poets Addicted To Moths

for Bill Kemmett

Moth of innocence
Moth of consciousness
Moth of shoes and IQ
Moth of spare change and hello
Good-bye moth
Moth of tomorrow
Moth of red white and blue
Moth of purpose
Moth of metaphor and symbol
Moth of God
Moth of Satan
Moth of moths
Moths in closets
Lots of moths
Hundreds of them
Polyphemus   Cecropia   Hawk   Sleepy Underwing   Luna
Moths and mothballs
Moth of names
Moth of criticism and attitude
One-way street moths
It-takes-two-to-tango moths
Dada moths
Sound moths
Hip-hop rappin' 'til you're blue in the face moths
Moth of Hollywood
CIA moth
Rabid dog barking moths
Moth of beer
Moth of tolerance
Moth of incontinence
Beautiful moths on screens

Gangs of moths around street lamps
Midget moths
Ghost moths
Man in the grey flannel suit moth
Moth of simplicity
Moth of infinity
Never mix an abstract moth with a concrete moth
Ezra moth
Moth of delusion
Moth of pills and hemorrhoids
Moth of rain and sick leave
Mountain man moth
Moth of lightning
HEY YOU LEAVE THEM MOTHS ALONE MOTHS
Automatic writing moth
Cut it out already moths
My brother's nickname is moth
Stop it I mean it moths
Moths of comedy
Migraine moth
Chthonian and Apollian moths
Once there was a moth in orbit around my exwife's head
Pet moth
Talking head moth
Moth of sorrow
Get rid of the bum moth
Moth of combat
Trickster moth
Moth of climax and insecurity
Moth of insouciance
Hit the road jack moth
And don't you come back moth
No more moth
No more moth
No more moth
No more

Edvard Munch,
Edvard Munch

The green letters are UP.
The green letters are DOWN.

The green letters are DOWN.
The green letters are UP.

The green letters are fast
and come out of nowhere.

This is so important I scream:
Edvard Munch, Edvard Munch.

Airport Poem

Headaches in the drawers of time
Quick   babies running through airports
have curly-blue souls
Without pen or consciousness
I wait for the birds of love

Three shoes   two touchdowns   a memory
Sounds in my head
like carpenters pounding nails
into videos
I'm a whirlwind of experience
Resumé with orange sauce on it

My narrative begins with a loss of identity
I don't know the body
The doctor looks through a magnifying glass
and writes "seborrheic keratosis"
on a pad of paper with his address

Newspapers report the loss of ozone
I'm melting like wrong attitude wax feathers
It's no use to talk of a Wilderness Of Malls
Fingertip skills of the next century
How it will be possible to click on computers
and delete genes not to our liking
off of DNA molecules

Cold Feet

The idea negates an antifreeze fetish
Look in the pill jar for the consciousness pulleys
This waste of time
There's a mountain
There's a stone
The man who rolls the moon into his garage and disappears
Say "scrambled egg"
Recall the night of reciting the names of dried flowers
Yes   the fragmentation arrow is powered by automatic quivers
Just don't look up
A star is about to nova
Cross outs in the dissonant letter to the construction site
We have politicians willing to bite the cathode-ray tube
O jargon sleep eases its way into bones
Let's complicate
Complex the vortex
The image
The style of shoes after two-tones went out
Like I said to the deprogramming officer
Give me a nonsense syllable in an electrostatic field
(I'm the average guy
About 5' 9"
Weigh around 172 lbs.
Watch 28 hours of tv per week
Drink 11 beers Sunday — Saturday
Got married around 26 years old)
And I'll rewrite the history of the world

Greenhorns

Mom makes sandwiches with butter
and without.
I take the ones without.

The President is shot
and a student runs down the hall
smiling and screaming:
"The President's been shot!"

"Aren't you going to watch it
on tv?
It's on tv," my sister says.

I bounce my basketball up the street.
I'm thinking about the dance
and Kathy's tits.

Is it wrong?

They make us swim in the nude in gym class.
They make fun of those
who are afraid of the water.
In the shower my balls shrivel into atoms.

They call us greenhorns
and knock the books from our arms.
A punk picks me up and throws me
headfirst into a snowbank.

When the girl next to me
gets her period

during English class
the teacher locks us in the room
and calls us animals
through a small window in the door.

Dad drives a Bonneville.
The country mourns.

I want to be a gym teacher.

Pop Culture

for X. J.

The big intellects arrived in a boat
of Chinese ideograms

This morning
I
punctured
my index finger
on a staple
in a bag of
chocolate chip cookies

We talked about coherence

and loosely
coupled

organizations How it might
be possible
to arrange our "phrase finds"
into a palace
of breathtaking opportunities

Then she took up literary criticism
on the guitar
I admit I let the map of associations
fly out the car window

as we shared an exchange
about "the" pronoun
while driving

in the breakdown lane at sunset
Wine as a metaphor

of new life
is the purple sea
in our wax-paper Dixie cups
Suppose you were sitting
in a fifties diner

and the assigned poem
had to do with Americana   Would
you go with Elvis or be one of the boys
in a house of unamerican activities

Proper Ventilation

A farm interrupted answered
the hat on the phone.
A cadillac with tens and twenties
stuck in creases covered with tarp and guarded.
All night long he breathes funny
and looks for the looker inside of him.
And there are two poems: one with
laundry hung inside the house; the other
with it on the line out back.
He would like to flow.
How many times can this be repeated?
Original friends drop by to smoke.
Sudsy rivulets head for the sewer.
Drop your duds and make suds
his grandmother ordered.
Sugar cookies in the jar with red top
underneath the sink.
The memories and the guy with a stick
in the dirt feel out of focus.
Unmake the thing for Christ's sake.
Static. Noise. Departure.
A blue body (under a white sheet
beside an open window with wind
ruffling the curtains and light)
is all I remember.

Customary Strangers

I was reading poems about his mother
when the tractor-trailer burst into the yard
and crushed my hosta plants.
His mom could shoot a mean game of pool:
always wore a red party dress (décolleté)
when sinking the eight in the side
and thinking of the Sunday pot roast.
I knew the trucker had been drinking
in a small town with a single bar
run by a man with a bullet
lodged in his jaw
who kept a python in a shed
with a John Deere mowing tractor
and mementos from the days
his son played with toy explosives
before joining the army
to destroy bridges of bad ideology
springing up in the world
like fleurs du mal.

The trucker insisted there was a road
inside my house
and if I consented to hop in his truck
he'd let me shoot holes
in deer crossing signs
as he roared down my living room
blowing retreads and tripping
alarms in the canvases
of two twentieth century masters
I'd stolen while drunk on wine
from a rich girlfriend.

I felt no remorse about the theft
suspecting from my days in the factory
I had missed a turn or two
and with a hatred for customary strangers
maps or the desire to go back
probably had detoured onto a path
littered with failed campaigns
and remnants of escape.
Things beyond the ken of poems
doused with twilight
and pinned on the backs of human targets.

When the trucker yanked on his horn
it was my chance to find out.

For Beer

so he threw the artist out
with the bath water
and wondered what that
could mean. when the sidewalk
turned into a rainbow of flesh
he backpedaled through
the cracked yolk of philosophy.
he toyed with syntax on guitars
rolled his mouth up his face
like a sinner's stone
sweated emphatic lemons
and howled.
there were things to refer to:
the planet was on fire
and the fact of how
a butterfly in the Amazon rainforest
could alter the weather
by the flap of a single wing
created his craving for beer.
he wanted to wash out
the socks of others
and remember the hammer
in his Dad's hand
on hot days.
he preferred the odor of pine
but was caught in the shade
eating petals of blue sage.

Fragments of Glance and Odor

Because it's a dream
there's a lobster in my coffee
and I'm in Mexico
at a table
with an old man
who nods, smiles, drops harmonica
and dies when I show him
the cockroach on my sugar spoon.
It touched my lips
so I take it to the man and woman
behind the counter
who shield their eyes
from sun on my face
and exclaim: "it's no cockroach,"
but a lobster
which grows suddenly larger
and I see how the orange-black shell
grips the white tail flesh
and when I ask
"how can a lobster fit inside a coffee cup,"
the man kicks a grey water tank
and says: "this is where
we store water for coffee,"
and laughs about the lobsters
moving around inside of it.
Because it's a dream
I search my subconscious
to find you
to confirm my love
because I've been damaged
by weather and days

and need the fragments of glance and odor
to burst into the woman
who's told me of the times ahead:
how I will sit on a porch facing the sea
rocking with a quilt on my knees
and she will be there
when I scream out and fail to remember
what it was I wanted to remember.
Because it's a dream
I speak with wind in trees
as my voice.
I'm alone
an ocean-battered rock
with a colony of birds
for thoughts.
I need your lips
the speed of your body on top of mine
the signature of eyes up in smoke.
I don't care if things change
we're free
to step from bones
into grains of sand
calling us.
Because it's a dream
I'm hooked to image:
cockroach — lobster
love — sea
in desert light we dash
across highways.
I don't want prophets to reset alarms.
The morning waits outside my ears like a bus.
There's a flash of newspapers
a man looking for keys
when you enter the café
and order a cup of coffee.

Out There

the simultaneity of
there
perception becomes phrase
phrase
has meaning
lacks one
which is the
world
     by moment
of sunlight
     on hybrid
oaks
and the voice
of leaves
to secret
self
  as blackbird flies
in blue sky
over trees
      and news
about century's
exhaust finds
nervous pedestrian
by window
while the happiness
of dogs
barking at children
persists

Landscape of Fine Wine

for Charles Bernstein

Drop the "a" in apple
    on the sweetheart mandela
Eden skies swish by before the show
    of force at the new theater
Declarations by ducks at half-time
Get ready for the automatic parade
    of tellers   Puff the magic
mushroom said the fired D.J. to his
    penpal the Bridge a
        loose cannon from the
halcyon days
        OK professor with words
and waterfalls
        for pockets
    do we skip the introduction
        or rent the rented truck
    for the convention
        of applause malls
This is the space of memory
        the shape of energy
            the tension of molecules
in the Bubble Bath chamber
    of birth   Sentence after sentence
with meaning
        locked in a private joke
    outside the port-a-john
But the sun shines and the horse
    prancing through the
    window of contrivance knows the
    secret alphabet
        of stars and numbers

Say so   Say so   Say so   Just to say
                 So
              Language
          swims upstream
       in a salmon hurricane

(Do you have a pen I could borrow)

           Pies are squared before
                 the triangle admits
              to theft   He eats
           the beef before shouting
        to Mom   that he's OK
           Imitation is the highest
           form of fattery (1)   "Eats"
           the diner sign flashes
              deep into the night   The
        appearance of neon cacti
           scared the populace
              into fat-free chips
The doctor of news has
           a headache
           and message for the faithful
        left in the
           rain outside
              the revival tent
     Surrealism speeds
        through Einstein's
  dream of riding an arrow
              of light   Verify
              facts with footnotes
        or accept the
           wrath of teachers
              with gout   Curt
     Gowdy was a

            sports announcer
All's unfair in love
       and war
  The cliché maker tags the foot
    that's it   The old priest hobbles
      thru the narrative of the
          young poet confessing   After
          ten years of disordering
        the senses she
          called the sky
        a cow   The pleasure
          of being
            buried in
          the lost and
            found box
            raises like
                      eyebrows
            when the
            magician of
              verbs orders
          wine by the glass
          for his next illusion

(and you listen to people and those
postponing games pass thru radar undetected)

What I Am

I am out there
lost
gone
hopelessly demented
bonkers
crazy
abnormal
neurotic as the first
fertility goddess
I need help
I hear voices
stars
streams
nightmares
children crossing the street
horses chewing apples
nipples praying
insects fucking
toilets flushing
cocks crowing
grass growing
I have gone over to the other side
I've crossed the tracks
pupils dilated
I'm cracked
psychotic
schizo
bloodthirsty
there's not enough glue
in the glue factory
to keep me together

to appear
coherent
in public
calm
self-assured
saying the world is okay
it will be fine
in the morning
all it really needs
is a good night's sleep
a proper diet
a lousy break for Christ's sake
I am bizarre
insane
beyond electric shock
the pills don't help
the long talks on the couch
to find forbidden
events
have come up empty
I am a complex
instinctual baboon
torn by love
shredded by death
perverse
polymorphous
I like to suck my
toes
in front of security
cameras
I fondle meat in front
of butchers
I am cuckoo
a strange bird
in a foreign tree

with vulgar song
I am up before dawn
up before midnight
I am on the prowl
I mean no harm
everything scares me
I am out there
in the world
with you

Wake-up Call

The wilderness between wild places
X is not X
the past flowers

I was young as a bullet
in a silencer of tears and soda cans
saga of sundown streets

Chemical equations assuage cats
licking indigo shadows
cast by party hats

Left right left
kneel down
confess

something
anything
the material presence of effervescence

Do da Do da
filaments of rain on intestinal highways

Your "To Do List"
the histrionics of it
when history coughs rose

Fluke Of Insolvency

this morning (meaning any random morning)
the world awoke without money.
during the night (meaning any random night)
the money disappeared from the face
of the earth.
though the face seemed more radiant
a world without money
was hard to swallow.
those who had gone to bed with their pockets full
of the stuff
found not a single coin
when they awoke. most panicked
when they discovered homes and cars
were devoid of the signs and symbols
that provided the feeling
objects were worth something.
now they weren't sans explanation.
a few unlucky souls began to see
the trees, rocks, and minerals
their things were made of
and took sick; some died on the spot
when they caught a glimpse of something mysterious
and unattached to the concept
of value. it was a tough morning
for personal ownership.   those who scurried
to banks to check on life savings
were dismayed to find fields of tall wild flowers
had replaced financial institutions.
in the fields were birds of every color and beak-shape
busy at breakfast.   it was a horrible day

of the brightest light.
the people cried in the freshest breeze:
our stocks and bonds have become the clouds
above our heads.   oh, it sickens
us to see how white
and innocent they appear.   without a doubt
it was the greatest upheaval in a long time
with a few old minds
comparing it to the big bang
of adam's rib.

Who's There

you wanted freedom

there was a flower
to pick

was it truth
or heresy

then the stream
bark
woof-woof
all that

conversation
principle
form

those with pens
those with rakes

the luxury
of riding around
with the top
down

toot-toot

hair blowing
deep kiss
of blood

in the veins

clouds opened
(says-a-me)
improvisation
of wind
be-bop temples

cathedrals
fount of mistakes
what's right

the object
of course

its beauty
mystery

process

knock-knock

This Hand

It's not complete meaning
this phrase of time
you sing to me on feet
cute as bare ass

I've been to the school
of monkeys and know
dawn ripples like muscle
when we kiss   Now Venus

in frigid sky collapses
under the lonely weight
of blankets   I'm screaming
again   Out of my skull

like a soul whose search
for body lends the sea
its tiny wave   Walk on
dreams to grab this hand

Come Home

The convention of dark minds
took place
on the chameleon's back

The convention of light minds
took place
on the chameleon's back

After sessions of colorful opinions
dark minds turned light
light minds dark

And the wind blew
and trees whispered
to the chameleon

Evening Sky

a quiet brain
without the rage
of memories

still
an arrow not
in flight
as clock
strikes number

two eyes
home at last

The Sacristy Of Desire

We whisper
dark trees
in the
yard are
dizzy with
snow. I
mention your
beauty then
jump out
of bed
like a candle. So
it's time
to count
to one hundred like
a child
with a knack for
mistakes
and
blueberries. The
shifting silk
of dreams
flares red
in the
winter punch.

So much
to construct
to drag
into place
like a pyramid.   O
the magic
of carpets
swaying floors
when the mind recalls
the grammar
of stance.
Let's dance!

Next Sound

for Maureen Owen

If you listen to them   the sun
moon down steps into water   you might recall
the husky voice   a grey evening's wrong number
this talk between stars   and a mother's complaint
when she catches you burning
like a match in biblical darkness   It is

arrangement of sound that makes the street
look like a swarm of newspaper buses   beep
the men on the stoops with their staring tattoos
the woman who asks for fifty cents
will ask again   twinkling with history   the mind
knows what's phony and takes a breath
o this anger at metaphors and speed
the sloppy sluice of synapse juice   good morning
afterall   chips of clouds begin to fall

I'm tied of themes   nickels tossed into the air
heads/tails   you go first/you come last
that's the way it is in the House of Cliché
I'm pounding on the drums of what I hear
listening for something else   my ear bends
like space around planets   for the next sound
I'm rolling down an incline of future
to meet you sweet syllable   my hammock swings